To our favorite
science teacher,
Mrs. McCutcheon,
from
Valerie, Tobi, and Alicia

~

December 1998

SCIENCE SURPRISES

by Sandra Markle
Illustrated by June Otani

SCHOLASTIC

New York   Toronto   London   Auckland   Sydney

ISBN 0-590-48401-X

Text copyright © 1996 by Sandra Markle.
Illustrations copyright © 1996 by Scholastic Inc.
All rights reserved. Published by Scholastic Inc.

12 11 10 9 8 7 6 5   6 7 8 9/9 0 1/0
Printed in the U.S.A.   40
First Scholastic printing, September 1996

Contents

Introduction

Can you guess what will happen when you —

—huff and puff and try to blow two balloons apart?

—hold a Ping-Pong ball over a blow-dryer that is set on "high"?

—try to grow a bean plant in the dark?

—race a can of tomato soup against a can of chicken noodle soup?

Get ready to be surprised!

These and the other surprising activities in this book are fun to do at home. All you need are some materials you will find around the house or can buy cheaply at a grocery, hardware, or hobby store.

The activities will prove that science is full of surprises. And there are some "real-life science surprise" stories to amaze you, too!

REMEMBER

- **Do NOT do any activity involving a hot stove or a sharp tool without an adult to help you.**

- **Clean up the work area after you finish your project.**

- **Have fun!**

Make a Drop of Water Move Wood

Does it seem impossible for you to move anything with a single drop of water? Well, you can, once you know the science facts. In fact, with just a drop of water, you can move toothpicks into a star shape without touching them!

YOU NEED:
- ❏ A box of wooden toothpicks
- ❏ A sturdy plastic plate or a metal cake pan
- ❏ Water
- ❏ An eyedropper

Start by breaking five wooden toothpicks in half—but do it gently, so the wood fibers still connect the two halves together.

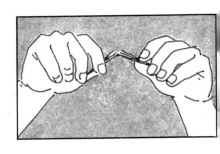

Bend each broken toothpick to form a V shape. Place the V-shaped toothpicks on a flat, smooth surface, such as a plastic plate or a metal cake pan. Arrange them in a circle so the points of all the V's are touching.

Now use an eyedropper dipped in water to drip one big water drop on the toothpicks. Be careful to have the drop land right on the spot where the points of the V shapes meet.

Surprise! The sides of the bent toothpicks begin to spread apart and the points move away from the center. A star forms all by itself!

Do you wonder how the water drop could cause this action?

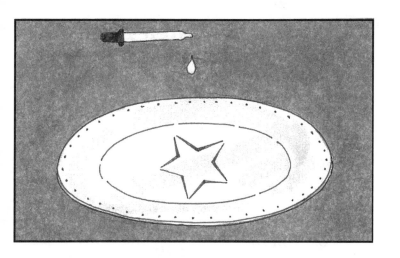

WHY IT WORKS

Take a close look at the fibers sticking out of the broken end of one of the toothpicks. The water was *absorbed,* or soaked up by these fibers just the way it's soaked up by a sponge. And just as a dry sponge becomes soft and flexible when it's wet, the wood fibers become more springy.

You can see for yourself how much springier the wood becomes simply by bending a dry broken toothpick and then bending one of the wet ones.

Now think about this. Could you create a pentagon—a shape with five sides, as on a soccer ball—if you add more than one drop of water at the point of each V? Predict why you think this might, or might not, work. Then break five new toothpicks and test your prediction.

11

Can You Send a Penny into Orbit?

Sure you can. You make it orbit inside a balloon! All you need to do is apply some *centrifugal force*. How do you do that? Follow these steps.

YOU NEED:
- ❑ **A large balloon**
- ❑ **A penny**

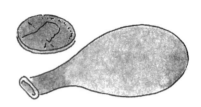

First, slip the penny through the neck of the balloon.

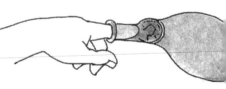

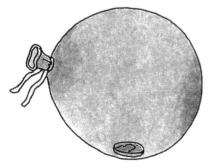

Blow up the balloon and knot the neck to seal it. (You may want to get help from an adult partner for this.) Next, hold the balloon and begin to move it so the penny inside is circling just as if it were on a race track. You will be moving the balloon very quickly around and around in a small circle. Guess what?

You're applying centrifugal force!

WHY IT WORKS

Centrifugal force is a force that propels something outward from a certain point. In this case, the centrifugal force you're applying is slinging the penny away from you. Because the coin is inside the balloon, though, it can go outward only until it reaches the balloon "skin."

Now, suddenly stop moving the balloon. The penny will keep on orbiting for a few seconds. Why? Momentum, the force of its motion, keeps the penny going.

But the friction of rubbing against the balloon slows the penny down. So does gravity, the force that pulls everything toward the earth. When it's no longer moving fast enough to keep going around, the penny drops out of orbit.

☆ EXTRA CHALLENGE ☆

Now use centrifugal force to make water stay in a plastic bucket, even when it's upside down!

Do this outdoors on a warm day. And just in case you don't succeed on the first try, wear a bathing suit.

Find a lightweight plastic bucket with a sturdy handle. Be sure you can swing it easily, moving your arm in a big circle.

After you have practiced moving the bucket fast through one big circle, pour water into the bucket until it is half full.

Now swing the bucket in a big circle again. As with the penny in the balloon, centrifugal force will sling the water away from you—long enough, in fact, for the water to remain in the bucket while it's upside down.

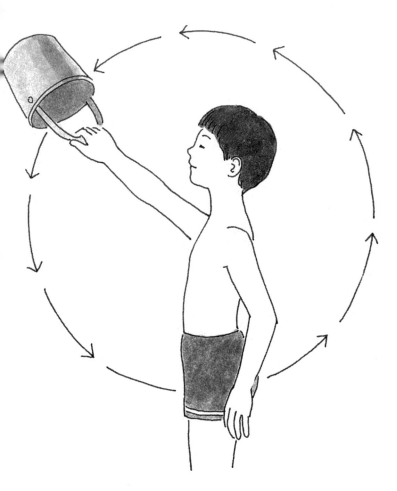

BUT if you move too slowly, gravity will take over. Guess what will happen to you if you are between the water and the earth's surface?

A Real-Life Science Surprise

Picture Perfect

Louis Daguerre

A long time ago, the only way people could have a picture of something was to have an artist draw one. Then, in 1835, a French painter named Louis Daguerre (say **da-gare**) discovered a way to make photographs that would last, and he did it quite by accident.

The first camera had been invented years earlier. It had a lens in one end of a box and a glass plate at the other end, where the image was focused. To make a copy of the image, a piece of paper was placed over the glass, and someone traced the image with a pen.

Daguerre used chemicals to try to make light entering the camera create a permanent image on a metal plate. His best results were with highly polished silver-plated copper plates that had been exposed to the chemical iodine. Any area where light struck the iodine changed to silver, creating an image. But the picture was very hard to see.

Then, one day, Daguerre put one of his "photos" in a cupboard, planning to clean the plate later and use it for something else. A few days later, when he took the plate out of the cupboard, he was amazed to see a clear picture!

This camera from 1839 was used to make Daguerrotypes.

Daguerre figured this had to be the result of fumes from some chemical in his cupboard. So he tested all the chemicals, one by one. No luck. Then he took the chemicals out and placed another photo in the empty cupboard. It developed just like the first one!

Finally Daguerre discovered the secret chemical that caused his photos to develop. On one of the shelves in the cupboard, he found a broken thermometer dripping mercury. Sure enough, when he made a test using mercury, a photo developed.

Daguerre had invented the first method of photographic processing, and his pictures, called Daguerrotypes, quickly became very popular.

Go Away, Penny!

Show your friends this science surprise, and let everyone take turns making the penny go away.

YOU NEED:

❑ **Six pennies**

Line up the pennies on a smooth table top. Place them so they are just touching.

Now move one of the end pennies about two inches away from the line.

Take careful aim, and flick your finger into the penny hard enough to drive it into the line of pennies. (If you miss at first, keep trying.)

When you strike the row of pennies—presto! The coin at the very opposite end will slide away from the line. It happens every time. Why?

WHY IT WORKS

When you flicked the penny, you gave it momentum, or propelled it forward, at a set speed. That momentum was stored up as it passed through the line of pennies. There was just enough momentum to move one penny, and that's what happened.

Can You Make a Can Roll Back to You?

Absolutely! You just need another way to store energy. To make a roll-back can, follow these steps. (You need an adult partner for this activity.)

YOU NEED:

- ❑ An empty coffee can, nut can, or similar can with a snap-on plastic lid
- ❑ A second plastic lid that fits the can
- ❑ A marking pen
- ❑ Sharp scissors
- ❑ Two long rubber bands
- ❑ Paper clips
- ❑ 10 to 12 metal washers
- ❑ String

First, ask an adult to cut the bottom out of the can with a can opener. *Be careful when handling the edges of the can.*

With the marking pen, put a dot in the center of each plastic lid.

Ask your adult partner to carefully poke two holes in each lid with sharp scissors. Make one about an inch above the dot and one about an inch below the dot.

Next, get two identical long, sturdy rubber bands and four paper clips. The rubber bands need to be as long as the length of the can *without* being stretched.

Then get 10 metal washers and thread them onto a piece of string about eight inches long.

Now you are ready to put together your magical roll-back toy.

DO THIS: Snap one lid onto the can.

Poke one rubber band through each of the holes of this lid.

(If the holes are too small, have your partner make them larger.)

22

Slip a paper clip over each rubber band so it can't pull back through the hole.

While your partner holds the other lid, poke the ends of the rubber bands through the other two holes, crossing the rubber bands so the one attached to the lower hole of the first lid goes out the upper hole of the second lid.

Anchor each end with a paper clip.

Now for some real teamwork! Hold the lid open slightly, while your partner reaches inside and ties the center of the two rubber bands together with a small piece of string . . .

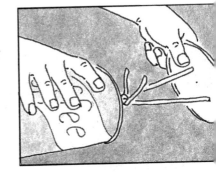

. . . and then ties the string of metal washers onto the center of the crisscrossing rubber bands so that the washers hang down.

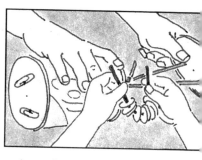

Snap the lid in place, and you're done!

It's time for a test roll.

Use a level, smooth surface for best results. Give the can a gentle push to roll it away from you. It should travel a short distance, stop . . . and roll back!

If the can does not return or does not roll all the way back, check to make sure the rubber bands are loose enough to wind up inside the can. Tie more washers to the center of the rubber bands, if necessary. Then try again.

WHY IT WORKS

The roll-back can works because the center weights make the rubber bands twist. Rubber bands are elastic, meaning they can change shape under force and then return to their original shape. So, as the can rolls, the weight keeps the center section of the rubber bands from turning. As a result, the rubber bands twist, and in doing so, they store some of the energy of your push. When the can stops rolling forward, this stored energy makes the rubber bands unwind, sending the can rolling in reverse.

☆ EXTRA CHALLENGE ☆

How far can you get your can to roll away from you and then return?

Ask your partner to mark how far the can goes before it reverses so you can measure the distance. Brainstorm to think of things you might try to make your can roll even farther and come back. Test the idea you think is most likely to work.

A Real-Life Science Surprise

A Hot Discovery

Charles Goodyear

Rubber got its name because it could rub out pencil marks. But until Charles Goodyear discovered a way to improve rubber in 1839, nobody thought it was good for much else. Rubber became too soft and sticky when the weather was warm and too stiff and brittle when the weather was cold. Goodyear, though, was impressed with rubber's good qualities, especially its stretchiness.

Charles Goodyear was an American inventor. He was sure there had to be a way to fix rubber so it wouldn't be affected by temperature changes. In 1830 he began to experiment. His efforts went on during the next nine years, using up nearly all his family's money. And working with chemicals nearly ruined his health.

At one time, Goodyear thought he had solved the problem, and he got a government contract to use rubber to make waterproof mailbags. But as soon as the bags got hot, they became sticky.

Then one day, while he was mixing some rubber with a chemical called sulfur, Goodyear accidentally let the mix-

Charles Goodyear worked long hours in his laboratory in Woburn, Massachusetts. His experiments led to many useful rubber products, from waterproof boots to automobile tires.

ture touch a hot stove. The rubber charred, but it didn't melt. Imagine how surprised and happy Goodyear felt! Even better, after being left outdoors in the cold winter weather, the burned rubber remained flexible and stretchy.

Goodyear called his rubber-treating process vulcanization after the mythical Roman god of fire, Vulcan. He never got rich from his discovery, but it led to the manufacture of many rubber products. The biggest use came later, when rubber tires were developed for automobiles.

Can You Guess
Which Way the Air Will Go?

What if you could hook together two balloons—one blown up only a little and one almost fully blown up—so the air could flow between them.

Which way would the air go? Would it flow from the bigger balloon to the smaller one until both were nearly the same size? Or would the air flow from the smaller balloon into the bigger one?

Guess what you think would happen, and why. Then follow the directions to test your idea. (You will need some help from an adult partner.)

YOU NEED:

❑ Two "jumbo" balloons (16-inch size)
❑ A plastic film can from a roll of 35mm film, without its lid (usually free for the asking from stores that develop film)
❑ Sharp scissors
❑ Two medium-sized binder clips

Ask an adult partner to "drill" a hole in the bottom of the film can with the scissors. The scissors should be twisted back and forth to enlarge the hole.

Blow up one balloon until it is inflated to about twice its uninflated size. Twist the neck to seal the balloon, and have your partner hold the film can while you roll the neck of the balloon over the open end.

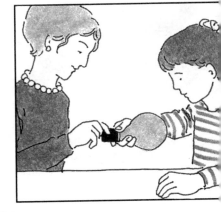

Keep the neck twisted, or use a clip to pinch it shut.

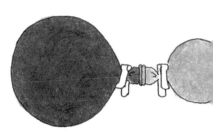

Now blow up the other balloon until it's nearly fully inflated.

Twist the neck as you did before, and slip the neck over the bottom of the film can (the end with the hole punched in it).

Get ready for a science surprise! Hold the film can in the middle between the two balloons. Have your partner carefully remove the clips.

Were you surprised that the air rushed from the balloon that is only slightly blown up to the one that is nearly full of air? Why does this happen?

WHY IT WORKS

The stretchy balloon material actually exerts some pressure on the air that's inside the balloon. The more air inside, the more the material is stretched and the thinner it becomes. And the thinner the balloon's "skin" is, the less force it exerts. (You probably noticed that it was harder to blow up the balloon at first, and it took less blowing force as the balloon expanded.)

Because there is more force being exerted on the air inside the less inflated balloon, the air was pushed into the larger, more fully inflated balloon.

The air stopped flowing out of the little balloon when the balloon shrank to about its uninflated size.

Can You Huff and Puff and Blow Two Balloons *Apart*?

What will happen if you blow between two balloons that are hanging so they're almost touching? Will the balloons move away from each other? Will they move toward each other? Or will they stay right where they are?

Make your prediction, and then follow these steps to find out what really happens. You need a partner for this activity.

YOU NEED:
- ❑ **Two identical round balloons**
- ❑ **Two pieces of string about 12″ long**

First, blow up the balloons so they are nearly fully inflated. Tie a string to the neck of each balloon.

Ask your partner to hold the balloons high so that they are almost—but not quite—touching.

Bend over or sit so that the balloons are at a height you can reach easily. Then blow between the balloons. Blow hard!

No matter how hard you blow, the results are the same: the balloons move *toward* each other instead of being blown apart. What a surprise!

WHY IT WORKS

This happens because fast-moving air has less air pressure. So the air you puff decreases the air pressure between the balloons. And this lets the air with greater pressure around the balloons push them together.

A Real-Life Science Surprise

The Case of the Clumsy Inventor

Hilaire de Chardonnet

In the 1870s, the French silk industry was in a panic. A disease was killing the silkworms, whose cocoons were the source of fibers used to spin silk thread. Louis Pasteur, the scientist noted for finding cures for human diseases, tried to save the silkworms. Working with him was his assistant, Hilaire de Chardonnet (say **Hee-lar duh shard-o-nay**).

Although Pasteur helped to solve the problem, Chardonnet decided that the best way to prevent any future problems was to come up with a man-made, or *synthetic*, substitute for silk.

He tried many ways to do this, but nothing worked. Then one day in 1884, he accidentally spilled a chemical while he was developing photographic plates in a darkroom. He couldn't stop just then to clean up the mess. And later, when he did get around to cleaning up, he got a surprise.

Rayon has been made in factories for a long time. This old photo shows rayon threads being wound onto spools.

The chemical he had spilled was called *collodion* (say **co-load-ee-on**), and the partially dried collodion formed long, thin strands as Chardonnet tried to wipe it up. These strands reminded him so much of silk that he tried to produce more.

It took six years of experimenting, but Chardonnet finally developed fibers strong enough to weave into cloth. This man-made "silk" eventually became known as *rayon*.

Check the labels of your family's clothes. It's likely that some contain rayon, because it's a very popular synthetic material. Rayon, like silk, has a sheen because its fibers are smooth. Today's rayons are made out of different chemicals from the one Chardonnet used, though. His rayon easily caught fire.

Can You Make a Ball Float in the Air?

What if you aimed a blow-dryer straight up at the ceiling and placed a Ping-Pong ball in the jet of air? When you let go of the ball, will it be blasted toward the ceiling? Will it stay suspended in the fast-moving air? Or will it drop to the floor?

Think about what could happen and why it's likely to happen. Be sure to consider what happened when you blew between the two balloons in the activity on page 33.

YOU NEED:

❑ A blow-dryer
❑ A Ping-Pong ball
❑ A balloon (optional)
❑ A tennis ball (optional)

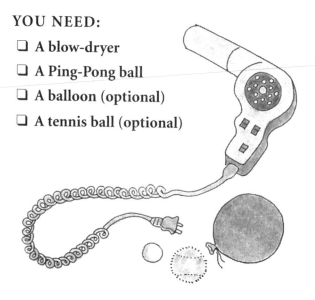

You may want to have an adult partner hold the blow-dryer for you, with the nozzle aimed straight up. When the dryer is switched on to "high," place the ball in this column of fast-moving air so it's about five inches above the nozzle. Let go of the ball and quickly take your hand away.

It's just like magic!

As long as the air current is shooting straight up, the Ping-Pong ball will float suspended above the dryer's nozzle. Of course, it isn't magic at all. It's science.

WHY IT WORKS

Fast-moving air has less pressure than more slowly moving air. So the Ping-Pong ball is trapped inside the column of fast-moving air. Here the ball is pushed upward by a jet of air with enough force to keep it from falling, but not enough to blow it any higher.

Do you think you could suspend a tennis ball in the jet of air? What about an inflated balloon? Think about the weight of a tennis ball and a balloon compared to the weight of a Ping-Pong ball to help yourself predict what will happen. Then test your predictions.

By the way, what you discovered is also the basic law of nature that helps airplanes fly. When viewed on edge, the upper surface of an airplane's wing is curved and the lower surface is flat. Air slips over a curved surface more quickly than it does over a flat surface. So there is less air pressure on the upper surface of the wing than there is beneath the wing, giving the airplane lift.

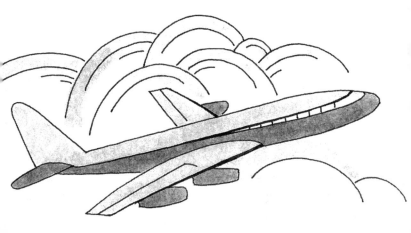

Can you guess why airplanes usually take off into the wind?

Can Water Crush an Empty Plastic Milk Jug?

It can. Watch what happens yourself. (You'll need an adult partner to work with you on this project.)

YOU NEED:

- ❑ **An empty gallon-size plastic milk jug with a snap-on lid**
- ❑ **A pan large enough for the jug to fit into easily**
- ❑ **An oven mitt**
- ❑ **A tablespoon**
- ❑ **The kitchen stove and sink**

First, fill the kitchen sink about two-thirds full of cold water.

Put about a table-spoon of water into the milk jug.

Pour water into the pan until it's about a quarter full, and heat just until it starts to boil.

Turn the heat down to low.

Have your adult partner use the oven mitt to put the jug into the boiling water and hold it there for one minute.

Then have your partner quickly lift the jug out of the boiling water, snap on the cap, and plunge the jug into the sink of cold water. The jug should be turned around and around so all the sides are exposed to the cold water.

When the jug is lifted out of the water you can see a big change! The sides will be dented. The jug may even look crushed.

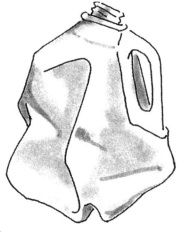

Why do you think this happened? Why do you suppose it was important to put water in the jug? Why was it important to put the cap on before plunging the jug into cold water?

WHY IT WORKS

Did you figure out that the answers to all of these questions have to do with *air*?

When the water in the pan was heated, you saw steam rising from the boiling water. Once it got hot enough, the water inside the jug turned to steam, too.

Then the steam drifted up, escaping from the jug and pushing out most of the air with it. Quickly capping the jug prevented any fresh air from replacing this lost air. Plunging the jug into cold water made any remaining steam condense, or turn back into water.

Water takes up even less space than steam. Without air or even water vapor inside the jug to push outward, the pressure of the water surrounding the jug was enough to push inward, denting or even crushing the sides.

A Real-Life Science Surprise

Up in Smoke

Sometimes nature packs a surprise, too. Imagine how you would feel if a volcano suddenly started erupting in your backyard!

That's just what happened in 1943 on a farm 200 miles west of Mexico City, Mexico.

Farmer Dionisio Pulido was plowing his cornfield when he saw glowing cinders popping out of a little hole. He tried to fill the hole with dirt, but he couldn't.

By the next day the little hole had become a pit nearly six feet across, and hot stones were being tossed higher than his head.

It was the birth of a new volcano, which was named Paricutín. Within one year, the volcano was a mountain 1,200 feet high. The cornfield was completely buried under molten rock (lava). So was the nearby town!

The volcano Paricutín was still active seven years after it started as a small hole in the middle of a cornfield. A few buildings, palm trees, and a dock remain standing in the shadow of the newly formed mountain.

Weird Plants You Can Grow

Want to grow some really weird plants? Then try this.

YOU NEED:

- ❑ Dry soup beans, such as kidney beans or great northern beans, from the grocery store
- ❑ A bowl of water
- ❑ Two small clay flowerpots or two Styrofoam cups
- ❑ Potting soil
- ❑ Clear plastic wrap

Pick out ten beans that are not cracked or broken, and put them in a bowl of water. Let the beans sit overnight.

46

The next day, fill two small clay flowerpots with potting soil. (If you use Styrofoam cups instead, poke a hole in the bottom of each one with a pencil first.)

Plant five of your soaked beans in each cup, poking the bean just beneath the surface of the soil.

Sprinkle with water so that the soil is damp but not wet.

Cover the pots with clear wrap and set each one on a saucer or small dish. (Do not use paper plates.)

Now place one pot in a sunny place.
Put the other pot inside a closet or cupboard.

 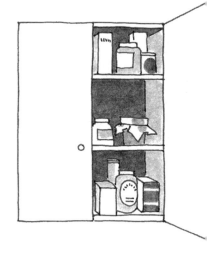

Every few days, lift the plastic wrap and sprinkle with water.

The beans should sprout within a few days. Keep watering and watch the young plants for about a week.

Are you surprised to see what's happening to the plant growing in the dark? It looks like it's going wild. The sprouts are long and thin. They are also strangely pale.

WHY IT HAPPENED

Don't worry. These beans have not become monsters. This is just what happens when they don't have enough light.

Normally, green plants need sunlight in order to produce a chemical called chlorophyll (say **klor-a-fill**). It's chlorophyll that makes the plant green. And the plant needs chlorophyll along with sunlight and water and carbon dioxide gas from the air to make food.

At first the young plant is able to grow even if it doesn't have sunlight or chlorophyll to make food. It uses the food that was stored inside the bean. If left in the dark, though, your weird plant will die.

Do you wonder what would happen if the plant was moved from the dark into the sunlight? Try it and find out.

A Real-Life Science Surprise

Yucky Stuff Becomes a Wonder Drug

Dr. Alexander Fleming

Dr. Alexander Fleming, a British doctor, tended soldiers on the battlefield in World War I. He wished there were a better antibiotic, or germ-killer, to treat the wounds. All he had available in those days was carbolic acid, and this acid also attacked the white blood cells, the body's natural defenders against the germs called bacteria (say **back-tee-ree-a**). So the cure often did as much harm as it did good.

After the war ended in 1918, Fleming set to work to find an antibiotic that would kill disease-causing bacteria without damaging the body's white blood cells. And one day, he did.

While suffering from a cold, he used his own nasal mucus to grow bacteria. And while he was examining this bacteria, a tear fell from his eye onto the plate. The next day, the spot the tear touched was free of bacteria!

Fleming was excited, but the bacteria-killing substance in tears didn't prove to be very effective against most disease-causing bacteria.

A few years later, in 1928, Fleming was doing research on influenza. He discovered that one dish of the bacteria he was studying had been spoiled by mold. He was about to clean out the dish when he noticed a clear spot. He remembered what had happened before with his tear.

When he looked closer at the mold, he discovered that the mold had killed the bacteria.

Fleming did some tests with the mold. To his surprise, this particular type of mold produced an antibiotic substance that could kill a number of different types of bacteria, including those responsible for some serious human diseases.

Fleming named the substance the mold produced *penicillin* (say **pen-is-ill-in**). And this antibiotic became known as a "wonder drug" because of the many lives it saved.

Taken in 1953, this photograph shows the culture plate that started the work on penicillin. "25 years old and rather dried up," Dr. Fleming wrote in his caption.

The Surprising
Soup-Can Race

Which of the two cans of soup do you think will reach the bottom of a ramp first—a can of chicken noodle soup or a can of tomato soup? Or do you think the race will be a tie?

YOU NEED:

❏ A board or a piece of sturdy cardboard three feet long and wide enough to hold two soup cans rolling side by side

❏ Waxed paper

❏ Clay

❏ A can of condensed chicken noodle soup

❏ A can of condensed tomato soup

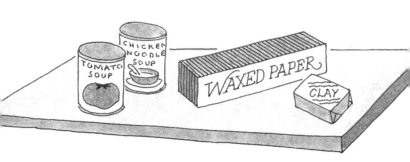

Prop up one end of the board about three inches. This will be your racetrack.

Make sure the race cans are identical in every way except for their contents.

Which one will win? You can predict the outcome, once you know what will be happening inside the cans.

To find out, cover the ramp with a sheet of waxed paper.

Then drip one drop of water at the top of the slope.

See how the water drop just slides down the ramp.

Do the same with a ball of clay. The clay rolls downhill.

HOW TO GUESS THE WINNER

Do not start your race yet, but think about this: At the top of the ramp, both cans will have exactly the same amount of *potential energy*—the energy that's available for them to roll downhill.

As the cans begin to roll, part of that potential energy will be used to move the can down the ramp. Part will be used to make the can go around and around like a wheel, because the can doesn't just slide forward, it rolls.

Inside the cans, the chicken noodle soup, which is mostly liquid, acts like the drop of water; the thick tomato soup acts like the ball of clay. The result is that some of the tomato soup can's potential energy is also used to make the soup go around with the can.

The chicken noodle soup, however, just flows downhill with the can, so more of the potential energy can go into propelling the can forward.

Now that you know all of this—guess which can of soup will win the big race. The tomato soup? The chicken noodle?

Get ready, set, go! Be sure the cans don't bump into each other along the track.

Try it again and again. Switch the starting places of the cans. You'll have the same winner every time.

For an extra challenge, select two different cans of soup that are identical except for the contents. Use what you learned to predict the winner of this race, too. Then hold the race to see if you were right.

Can You Prick a Balloon Without Popping It?

You can, but only with a little help from science and an adult partner.

YOU NEED:

- ❑ Several round rubber balloons
- ❑ A bamboo shish kebab stick. (These sharp sticks are inexpensive and available at grocery and party-supply stores. If you can't find a bamboo shish kebab stick, use a thin metal shish kebab holder, or the thinnest knitting needle you can find.)
- ❑ A little vegetable oil
- ❑ A measuring tape (optional)
- ❑ Tape (optional)

56

Blow up several balloons. Do *not* fully inflate them.

Tie a knot in the neck of each balloon to keep the air from escaping. (Or you can twist the neck around and tie it tight with a string or twist tie.)

Ask your partner to rub some vegetable oil all along the bamboo stick.

Now take a good look at one balloon. See how the balloon looks darker close to the neck?

Find the spot opposite the neck that looks darker too.

The reason they look darker is because the balloon isn't stretched quite as thin at these two spots.

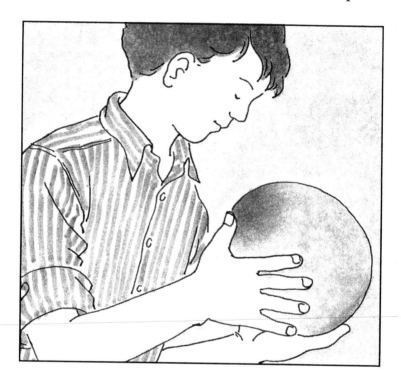

Now, have your partner insert the bamboo stick, pointed end first, into the dark spot close to the balloon's neck. It may help to slowly twist the stick as it is inserted.

The stick should be pushed through the empty middle of the balloon and come out through the dark spot opposite the balloon's neck.

CAUTION: Be sure the sharp end of the stick is pointed away from you and not aimed at anyone else, in case the balloon pops.

If the balloon does pop, coat the stick with more oil and try again with another balloon. With practice, your partner will succeed in skewering the balloon without popping it.

WHY IT WORKS

This surprising stunt is possible because the balloon is made out of a *polymer*. Polymers are giant molecules, made up of whole chains of molecules bonded together. When the stick slides into the balloon where these molecules are not stretched taut, it actually slips between the molecules. The stretchy material then clings tightly to the stick so the balloon doesn't leak and deflate.

However, if the stick is not slipped between the molecules and the material tears, the air inside the balloon escapes suddenly. *Pop!*

Do you find it hard to believe that the stretched material, or "skin," of a balloon is not solid? You can do a test to prove it.

Blow up a balloon so it's fully inflated, and tie the neck tightly. Then use a measuring tape to measure the distance around the balloon at its biggest point. Write down this measurement.

Measure the balloon again every day for a week. Surprise! The balloon shrinks as the air escapes between the molecules of the balloon's "skin."

☆ EXTRA CHALLENGE ☆

Do you think the trick would work better if you first reinforced the spot on the balloon where the stick is inserted with a piece of tape?

Predict why you think this might, or might not, work better. Then stick tape on the balloon and test your prediction.

A Real-Life Science Surprise

Sticky Discovery

Sometimes the surprise is just something that's noticed, making the inventor say "Whoa!" That's what happened in the early 1950s when George deMestral went for a walk in the woods and got cockleburs stuck to his jacket. Impressed by how hard it was to pluck the burrs off his coat, deMestral

took a closer look at the hooks covering these seeds. The hooks were nature's way of distributing the cockleburs, hooking them to the fur of passing animals.

DeMestral got the idea to develop tapes of looped thread and coordinating tapes of hooks to make fasteners. After many improvements, the combination of hooks and loops became Velcro. Today, it's

The idea for Velcro fastners came from the common cocklebur, a plant that grows in wooded areas.

used for everything from fastening shoes and coats to anchoring equipment aboard the space shuttle.

How many different ways can you think of in which Velcro is used?

The inventor George deMestral shows how Velcro works.

Photo credits: The Bettman Archive, page 35; Culver Pictures, pages 17 & 45; Hulton Deutsch/Woodfin Camp, page 50; Keystone Press, Zurich, page 63; Photo Researchers Inc., pages 51 & 62 (photo by Stephen P. Parker); Roger-Viollet, Paris, page 34; University of Akron Archives, pages 26 & 27.